LeBron James

*The Inspirational Story of One of
the Greatest Basketball Players
of All Time!*

Patrick Thompson

Table of Contents

Introduction

This book gives an insight into the life of LeBron James beyond basketball.

LeBron is one of the most recognizable sports figures in the world because of his remarkable athleticism and on-court brilliance. He dazzles sports fans with his flawless shots and powerful dunks. His dominance on the court is unlike any other. He has made and broken historic records in basketball and he continues to do so in more than 16 years of playing in the NBA. Even with a slew of new talents, LeBron still dominates.

The one thing the separates him from the other basketball superstars is his strong desire to win not just in basketball but in life. LeBron's off-court endeavors are as remarkable as his on-court performances. His incredible life story is a treasure trove of life lessons that inspire, motivate, and drive you to action.

This book paints LeBron James in a different light. Basketball is what made him a superstar, but it was his humble beginnings that shaped his ideas, moral values, and winning mindset. Knowing his story will make you see that he is more than just a basketball player chasing rings and winning ballgames.

Thanks for buying this book. I hope you enjoy it.□

Chapter 1

- The Pauper -

LeBron Raymone James always knew he was destined for greatness. The kid from Akron, Ohio had a rough start in life, being born to a teenage mother and an absent father. His difficult childhood didn't change his outlook in life. He was always optimistic and hopeful even when adversity followed him around like a shadow.

Born on December 30, 1984, to Gloria Marie James and Anthony McClelland, LeBron was already at a disadvantage early in life. Growing up in Akron exposed young LeBron to poverty and hardships. The difficulties were magnified by the absence of a father figure. His father had no interest in him and refused to be involved in his life. It proved to be a blessing in disguise because his father was in no position to take care of a child with his mounting criminal records.

Akron isn't exactly an ideal place for a single mother to raise a young son. The once-booming tire industry in the city crashed in the 1980s, creating a glaring economic disparity where the affluent got richer and the poor got poorer.

Lebron lived in the family-owned Victorian house near downtown Akron. Shortly after giving birth, his mother Gloria went back to school and left the child-rearing to Grandmother Freda. Unfortunately, Freda died of a heart attack when LeBron was just three years old. Things went on a downward spiral as the house fell into disrepair and bills started to pile up. It didn't take long for the eviction notice to come. The house was eventually torn down and Gloria and James were left to fend for themselves.

Being a teenage mom, Gloria had limited options. She had trouble finding jobs and when she found one, she had difficulty keeping the job. The lack of opportunity for a young mother forced the mother and son to move from one apartment to the next in the projects of Akron.

Over the next five years, they moved over a dozen times, which forced LeBron to change schools frequently. Because of the economic instability and the constant moving, LeBron's relationships and friendships were all fleeting. He became a transient student who could not form lasting relationships because he was always on the move wherever life's circumstances take him.

Even at such a young age, he was rolling with the punches. Though difficult, he was able to adapt to the unusual lifestyle. His mother worked at nights and would sometimes not go home for a few days. Left to take care of himself, Lebron had feared that he would one day wake up and not see his mother at all.

When Lebron turned seven, he and his mother were on the brink of being evicted again from their one-bedroom apartment in the housing project. By some divine intervention, local football coach Bruce Keller invited LeBron to his youth football team called the East Dragons. It was not just an invitation to play an organized sport, but it was also an opportunity to have something stable; something structured, which LeBron sorely lacked in his life.

LeBron was far too serious for his young age. He never smiled and the hardships showed in his eyes. He was closed off because he never really had the chance to be around kids his age for a long stretch of time. Football changed all that. For the first time in his young life, he was having fun. He was a natural at the sport and he loved the interaction. He made friends and bonded with Frankie, the son of Coach Frank Walker, Sr.

LeBron ended up staying the night with the Walkers because he had nowhere else to go. That one night extended through to the entire school break. When Lebron turned nine, he moved in with the Walkers with Gloria's blessing. She knew it was the best arrangement at that time because LeBron needed a permanent home so he could register for school. He had already missed most of the school year and he couldn't afford to miss the next year.

The Walkers decided to enroll LeBron at Portage Path Elementary together with their three kids. LeBron couldn't be a better kid in the Walker household. He was always helping out with the chores and staying out of trouble.

It was during his stay with the Walkers that LeBron learned to play basketball. The basketball net on the garage became a training ground for the young LeBron who developed a love for the game. Frank taught Frankie and LeBron the basics and soon moved on to more difficult dribbling drills and shooting layups with their left hands.

LeBron became frustrated when he couldn't shoot using his weak hand. However, he never complained. Instead, he practiced and practiced until basketball became second nature. Frank was impressed at LeBron's comprehension.

Everything he taught him stuck in his young mind. He was like a sponge that absorbed everything he could learn.

While LeBron adapted to the new family set up, Gloria made sure that she remained part of the family dynamics. She would visit on weekends to spend quality time with LeBron. Whatever money she had, she made sure that LeBron got it. She made LeBron feel that she was always there for her. Despite the distance, their relationship never soured nor faltered. They had each and other and that was all that matters.

LeBron was on and off the Walker home until 2002, the year he turned 17. He was already a junior year student at St. Vincent-St. Mary High School. With his prowess, he quickly became a basketball sensation. Tickets to his games were always sold out and had to be moved to bigger venues to accommodate more fans who were dazzled by LeBron's powerful dunks and Magic-like passing.

There was clamor for LeBron that's why ESPN aired his high school games nationally. In his national TV debut, he did not disappoint. He gave what people wanted because he was just that good. His transformation from a quiet young kid from Akron to basketball phenom was taking shape right before everyone's eyes. Some people doubted him, but he just kept playing and proving them wrong.□

Despite the new-found fame, LeBron's feet were firmly planted on the ground. Even when he got a new apartment, which he shared with his mother, he still visited the Walkers. He would still look for Frank during his games because he still valued his presence. Frank will always be the father figure that LeBron looked up to.

Although Frank taught LeBron the fundamentals of basketball, it was Coach John Reed who taught him how to be a basketball player. He was the one who instilled in LeBron the "team-first" mentality. He had told every player in his team that if someone is open, they should pass the ball.

It was the only way they could expand their game.

Because of the team-first approach, LeBron learned how to play every position in the team. He understood that no matter how tall he was, he had to know how to play the role of a point guard, small forward, or center. It was a way to work on the weakest part of his game. He would play post-up first, then work on his passing the next. He wanted to be an all-around player who can play any position.

The passing role was something that LeBron took seriously. He was already a gifted ball passer to begin with. But he was not one to be satisfied with what he could do. He didn't want to be just better; he wanted to be the best. That's just the way he was then, and still the way he is now. Nothing had changed. If anything, he became more competitive and more focused on his craft.

LeBron was only eight-years-old when Frank brought him to Coach Reed. Reed was then the head coach of the Summit Lake Hornets, where

Frank was an assistant coach. At that time, LeBron was still hopping from one apartment to the next. Reed got off from his work at the construction at 4 p.m. and picked up any kid who needed a ride to the Summit Lake recreation center for games or practice. He worked at the city's parks and recreation in the evenings.

Since LeBron had no permanent place to stay, he would call Reed or leave messages on his answering machines to let him know where he would be on a particular day. No matter which part of Akron's inner-city projects LeBron was, he would always be there waiting for Coach Reed to pick him up. He would show up wearing his jersey, shorts, and Converse high-tops. In the winter, he would be covered in a thick jacket. But no matter how cold or warm the weather got, LeBron would be waiting holding a worn-out basketball that was given to him by the coaches from Summit Lake. He took the ball everywhere he went. It was like an extension of his life. That was how committed he was at basketball. To some, it's just an after-school or after-work game, but to him, it was life. It was structure.

After a game or a practice, LeBron would stick around at the Summit Lake center and hang around with the other kids while waiting for Coach Reed to finish off his duties as the center's facility manager. When there were older players practicing, LeBron would try to join them. He would even play against older women players. As expected, LeBron could not compete with older players because he was just a little kid. He didn't have the experience that the older players had— they had played competitively against schools from other cities or other states.

LeBron hated losing. He always took it hard whenever his team would lose. He didn't consider the fact that he was the youngest on the court during pickup games. To him, his size and age were not an excuse to not be the best player on the floor. In his mind, whenever he's on the court, he had to be the best player.

His mindset had always been about improving his skills and becoming the best. He had the winner mentality that no other kids in the center have. Most of the kids were there to the hoop and had some fun, but LeBron was there to win. □

LeBron knew that if he worked on his basketball, he would be in the best shape to compete. The boy did his work. When he was not doing some shootaround in Summit Lake, he was hanging out with the older kids and adults at the big gym over at Elizabeth Park projects. He loved it there because it was a gym for adults who played pickup games. He felt that he was getting valuable training even though he rarely played.

Players who hung out at the Elizabeth Park gym would put their names on a sheet of paper and hoped that they would get picked up. LeBron would always write his name, but he rarely got picked by the older kids. Being the youngest kid, he was not taken seriously. He was always looked over and ignored. LeBron took the rejection to heart. He felt that they were doing it on purpose as a way to slight him. He was mad but he didn't cause any trouble.

LeBron kept practicing his shots and kept getting better at it; so much so that he was confident enough to challenge Coach Reed to a shooting competition after practices. Reed was good at shooting jumpers and he rarely missed his shots. LeBron was able to hit a few shots in a row but fell short to Reed's impressive shooting accuracy.

In one of their many shoot-outs, LeBron announced to everyone in the gym that he would beat Coach Reed and that he was going to the NBA. Such pronouncement was met with laughs and heckled from the volunteer coaches. Sure, they admit that LeBron had talent, but they were not convinced that he was built for the NBA. They thought that he had the talent for college basketball, but the NBA was a stretch. □

Coach Reed was flawless, but LeBron went shot for shot with him. When Reed finally missed and LeBron hit the final shot, everyone was astounded. LeBron then reiterated what he said, "I'm going to the NBA!"

This was a young boy who had nothing much in life but already knew what his future would be. Despite the hardships and difficulties in life, LeBron saw himself as a winner. In the face of adversities, he was optimistic and had a positive outlook on life. Instead of being defeated by the negativities, he used them as a motivation to improve his life's circumstances. He knew he was a winner right from the start and he would continue to have this mindset as he rises to the top.

Chapter 2
- The Phenom -

LeBron always knew what he wanted to achieve and he knew how to get it. He has always been calculating; always figuring out what works for him. When he was still a teenager, no one knew that side of him, but looking back at the decisions he had made in his life and career, one would see how everything he did in his days in the Akron league and AAU basketball foreshadowed what he did in the NBA.

LeBron the Phenom started to get some traction when Summit Lake Hornets defeated a rival squad that was touted as the Dream Team in the Akron recreation league. The Ed Davis Community Center team had a fearless point guard in Dru Joyce III. What he lacked in height, he more than made up for his intelligent and skillful gameplay.

21

The Hornet's victory over the Dream Team to win the city championship was a great feat for the young team and for Coach Reed. But the spotlight was pointed at LeBron who had a stellar game and scored 17 points and 5 assists. There was no mistaking that LeBron's celebrity status was on the rise.

Coach Reed recognized early on that LeBron was special. He had the talent for the game, but it was the way he worked on his skills that set him apart from other talented players in the league. When people didn't believe in his capabilities, he didn't engage in fisticuffs or acted like a self-entitled kid. He did the work—he worked on his jump shots, improved his passing, and communicated with his teammates. So, when he played on the court, he was electrifying. His detractors were proven wrong. He made believers of non-believers.

Whenever LeBron played, the team just automatically became better—the players played better and the gameplays were executed better.

Coach Reed admitted that his team was already good, to begin with, but LeBron made it exceptional. □

What's fascinating about LeBron is that even as a teenager, he could recognize talent from rival teams. He was secure enough in his abilities that he never thought of other great players as threats. Instead, he welcomed the great ones with open arms. Teaming up with them was an opportunity he sought.

Dru became LeBron's fiercest rival in the Akron league for two years. But it didn't stay that way long because the rivalry turned to an alliance when they joined forces in high school and in Amateur Athletic Union (AAU) basketball. In a way, this was a foreshadowing of the "recruiting" that LeBron has done in the NBA. He has been very vocal about his interest in playing with the best of the best in the league and such behavior can be traced back in his teen years.

LeBron recognized Dru's talent and considered

him an excellent basketball player. He wanted to be in the company of "All-Star" caliber players because he wanted to play with people who had the same winning mindset as he did. Teaming up with Dru was an easy decision to make.

From the people outside looking in, they would view this as getting talents to build a super team so that winning would come easy. What they didn't understand was that LeBron was showing his leadership skills early on. He was acknowledging another player's exceptional skills that would complement his own set of skills. It still takes a lot of hard work to win but having a leader that can recognize strengths and weaknesses among members of the team is the key to success. □

LeBron may be phenomenal on the court, but he was also exceptional in his insights about players. He would align himself with like-minded individuals who had the same goals and had the mentality to achieve them. He had been that way in his early years in high school and more so now in the NBA. One only has to look at how he had formed a solid alliance with Dwyane Wade and Chris Bosch in Miami to get back-to-back championships. The same is true with Kyrie Irving and Kevin Love to give the Cleveland Cavaliers their first-ever NBA championship. It's all a pattern of behavior that can be traced back in LeBron's teen years.

LeBron's rise to basketball supremacy has been etched in stone. The young phenom had already shown signs of invincibility and magnanimity in high school basketball. He had a commanding presence on the court and he appeared bigger than he was because of his powerful dunks that were indefensible.

Despite his growing popularity, his focus was still on the prize—the national championships. He never claimed that he could do it on his talents alone. He had adopted a team-first approach because that was what he was taught to do. He believed that basketball is a team sport and brilliant as he was, he needed help from his teammates.

LeBron had long credited his close-knit team from St. Vincent-St. Mary High School as the team that made him what he is today. They were five kids that rose to the challenge and fought all sorts of personal, emotional, financial, and psychological adversities to go all the way to the final game that would make them National Champions.

The five boys—LeBron James, Dru Joyce III, Romeo Travis, Willie McGee, and Sian Cotton— were the unlikely heroes that put St. Vincent-St. Mary to the high school basketball map. No one saw them coming. They were ranked last at one point in *USA Today's* super ranking.

With the help of Coach Dru Joyce (Dru's father), the Fighting Irish's starters changed high school basketball and elevated it to national consciousness. Many spectators attributed it largely to the basketball prowess of LeBron, but it was a team effort where each player played a key role to achieve success.

Not everyone knew the story of each of the boys. What they knew were the things they saw in the games or on television. They didn't see the difficulties and the hardships. Each of them had a heavy chip on his shoulder. They played through their struggles happening outside the court.

The boys all faced personal adversities, but instead of giving up, they were motivated by their unfavorable life circumstances. LeBron had no permanent home and no father figure. Little Dru had to prove to everyone that despite his diminutive size, he could be a great basketball player. Romeo was the outsider who was distant and had trust issues. Sian couldn't shoot to save his life. Willie had to deal with both of his parents' drug addiction. They were all battling something bigger than them. It was a difficult situation to be in at such a young age.

Even before they played basketball together, the boys had already bonded. LeBron was friends with Dru first because he was essentially living with Dru's family when they were in the sixth grade. They always played one-on-one games and LeBron would always beat the little guy. What LeBron liked about Dru was his "never give up" attitude. Even though he lost every single time, he just kept playing and playing until LeBron was forced to quit. LeBron was motivated by Dru's never-give-up attitude and it rubbed off on him.

Before playing for the Fighting Irish, LeBron and Dru played for the AAU travel team called the Shooting Stars. LeBron liked being around other kids and traveling around the city. His genuine curiosity and fascination about life made it easy for him to make friends.

Coach Dru recruited Sian Cotton for his formidable size and heft. It didn't matter that he was a baseball player and a lousy basketball player. The important thing was that he could intimidate other players with his fearlessness. He was a key piece in the dream team that Coach Dru was building.

LeBron, Little Dru, and Sian developed a

chemistry not just on the court, but off the court as well. They were bound to know everything about one another because they virtually spent their waking hours together. The long ride from Akron to Cocoa Beach, Florida for the AAU tournament became their bonding time. They knew each other like the back of their hands.

During their time together, LeBron learned more about their differences and it only made him appreciate their friendship. He recognized that Little Dru was a perfectionist. He became a great basketball player because he did the work. He honed his skills by repetition and by perfecting the drills. He had a work ethic of an adult and he worked doubly hard because he felt he had something to prove for being small. He wanted to get the respect that he deserved so he did the grind to make himself a force to be reckoned with.

LeBron learned from this because he didn't work as hard. He was a natural baller and he was great even with minimal effort. He developed the same fierceness and resilience that made his game better.

Sian was an unlikely basketball player. He was built for football because of his body. He was not a shooter, but he was a magnificent force on the defensive end. His presence in the paint was enough to intimidate anyone who dared go for a layup. However, his lack of skills in shooting frustrated Little Dru because every time he passed the ball to Sian, he would miss. It was a source of conflict, but they figured out how to make use of their strengths and worked on their weaknesses.

Willie McGee rounded up the Fab Four of high school basketball. He was from the West Side of Chicago, which was a tough place for a young kid. He was looked after by his sister because their parents struggled with drug addiction.

With a bad neighborhood and negligent parents, the lure of drugs and easy money was so strong. Without the guidance of his sister Makeba and his brother Illya, Willie could have easily lost his way and turned to a life of crime. He was lucky to have a great support system.

Had Illya not brought him to Akron one summer, he could have taken a different path in life. The trip from Chicago to Akron was the opportunity he needed to start anew and experience how to be a kid who can play and hangout with the good kids.

Spending time with Lebron, Sian, and Dru softened Willie's tough exterior. LeBron sensed that Willie shared the same love and passion for the game and that's what brought them closer together. LeBron always gravitated towards people who have the zest and passion for something that they really wanted to do—and in this case, it's basketball.

With Willie, LeBron saw resilience and toughness not just on the court, but in the face of adversity. He had much respect for Willie for being able to turn his back to the lure of the dark side.

LeBron could have easily been pulled to a life of crime, but he was smart enough to know the heavy consequences and the irreparable damage that it could cause to a young man with a promising future.

The Fab Four was committed to the game and they were hungry for the national championship. But they needed one more piece to the dream. That missing piece was Romeo Travis, a sophomore transferee from a public school. Because he had a falling out with the administration and the principal, he was discouraged from returning. □

LeBron was the only one who knew Romeo at that time because they went to middle school together. LeBron considered Romeo as a beast on the court. He was tall and tough with a jump shot. He had the height for blocking shots and he perfectly complemented Sian's defensive game.

It all seemed perfect, but Romeo was distant and reserved. It didn't help that he didn't want to be in Akron and he felt that the other kids don't want him there. Romeo's outlook had to do with his upbringing. He came from a broken family and he jumped from place to place and from school to school. This was not new to LeBron. If there was anyone who understood Romeo more, it was LeBron. They had a similar background, but the only difference was LeBron opened himself up to the concept of lasting and permanent friendship. To Romeo, friendship was fleeting, so he was not interested in building friendships.

The Fab Four and Romeo had all sorts of emotional and internal crutches going into the 2000-2001 season of the league. Despite this, they were able to advance to the Division III final four. They were flawless on the court, which attracted hordes of fans that reached close to 18,000. The boys of St. Vincent-St. Mary delivered and beat their opponent, the Miami East, convincingly.

LeBron was the real draw. Everyone wanted to

see the basketball phenom in action. Many wanted to see him succeed and some wanted to see for themselves if LeBron could live up to the hype. The kids knew that their every move was being watched and scrutinized. They felt an enormous pressure as a team, but they just played like they always used to with the guidance of Coach Dru, who had to take over as head coach after Coach Keith Dambrot left them for greener pasture in college basketball.

They learned to work with what they had—flaws and all. With the ragtag team of troubled teenagers, being national champions was a feat that the boys were proud of. Coach Dru knew the kids were good, but at that moment, he realized that they were special and were meant to do amazing things in their respective lives.

But things were different in LeBron's mind. Through all the hype and the publicity, LeBron was able to drown out the nice and introspectively assessed himself. Sure, he knew that all eyes were on him, but he never really lost sight of who he was, not just as a player, but also as a person.

LeBron was not only growing bigger, but he was also improving in his game. He was learning the finesse and the subtleties of the game. He was becoming what people expected him to be—a phenomenal basketball player who might just go straight to the NBA.

Chapter 3
- The Activist -

Getting into the NBA was the natural progression of LeBron's career as a basketball player. He lived up to the hype and even exceeded expectations. His achievements on-court are so great that many fans considered him the greatest of all time. While his being the "GOAT" is a highly debatable subject, his off-court accomplishments were set in stone.

LeBron is known for his philanthropic efforts, but his activism took its sweet time to come to the surface. To refresh one's memory, LeBron was adjudged as apathetic and apolitical when he side-stepped the highly controversial issue of the Darfur genocide.

Former Cavaliers teammate Ira Newble penned a letter criticizing the Sudanese government for the human rights violation and calling for a peaceful resolution of the armed conflict. It also asked China to stop supplying money and weapons to support the Sudanese government.

Many Cavaliers signed the letter in support of Newble's cause, but LeBron avoided the issue like the plague. Many became critical of his distasteful move. They called him ignorant, selfish, and self-absorbed. Many thought that a big celebrity athlete like him should use his power and influence to push for bigger causes and advocacies that could benefit people. He had the means and the platform, but he chose to be indifferent.

But that was 2007. Since then, LeBron had stepped up his activism and transformed into an outspoken advocate for the black community. His tenacity on-court extended off-court and he began to speak out about controversial issues and made a stand.

The transformation was gradual. He just didn't wake up one day realizing that he wanted to speak out on every political and social issue that affected him or his community. But the turning point was in 2012 when a black Florida teen Trayvon Martin was murdered by George Zimmerman.

The tragic incident hit a switch in LeBron because he thought of his own sons. He empathized with parents who had to deal with the loss of a son or a daughter to senseless killings perpetrated by racist thugs who stalked their preys. It made an impact on him also because the murder occurred in Sanford, Florida, which was near where he lived. At that time, LeBron was playing for the Miami Heat. Right there and then, LeBron realized that his powerful voice and his own platform could be used beyond sports. □

Before the cataclysmic event, LeBron only used his platform to endorse products and promote his personal brand. Every decision he made at that time was largely for economic gain and strengthening the LeBron James brand.

A few weeks after the incident, LeBron and his Miami Heat teammates appealed for justice for the murder of Trayvon. They were among the first professional athletes to make a strong and impactful statement about the killing. They showed their solidarity by posing in hooded sweatshirts. The picture went viral on Twitter and so did the hashtags #WeAreTrayvonMartin and #WeWantJustice. It was the start of LeBron, the activist and advocate.

Since that viral tweet, LeBron continued to serve as a voice and allowed political candidates to use his platform in support of social issues in pursuit of justice. He evolved not just as a player, but as a man who recognized the power that he wielded to change lives and influence outcomes. His LeBron James Family Foundation has expanded its goals to include fighting and advocating black rights.

LeBron spoke about controversial political and social issues without fear of reprisal from fans or sponsors. In 2014, he threatened to boycott the NBA if disgraced Los Angeles Clippers owner

Donald Sterling was allowed to become a team owner during that season. □

In a shocking interview with CNN's Anderson Cooper, Sterling attacked Earvin "Magic" Johnson and insisted that he had AIDS and set a bad example to the young people of Los Angeles. But what was more shocking was the idea of a LeBron James-less NBA. It was potentially damaging to the NBA should its biggest star refuse to play and take throngs of players with him. That was the power that LeBron wielded.

NBA Commissioner Adam Sterling didn't waste time apologizing to Magic Johnson and expediting the process to remove Sterling from the league as owner of the Los Angeles Clippers. While all this was happening, LeBron did not sit still. He kept protesting by wearing an "I Can't Breathe" shirt during warmups.

In 2016, LeBron used ESPYs as a platform to deliver a powerful speech voicing out the helplessness and the frustration that the black community and the nation feel about the senseless violence and killing of young black people.

Together with Chris Paul, Carmelo Anthony, and Dwayne Wade, LeBron challenged professional athletes to educate themselves about the issues and get involved in any way they can. His call to action was to invest time and resources to help rebuild communities that had been torn apart by violence and social unrest. He challenged everyone to stop the hate and the violence and urged everyone to do better.

It was a show of solidarity among basketball athletes and sports celebrities in light of the events of that year. It was a gutsy move that many did not expect from the basketball stars, more so from LeBron James, who had always been neutral and apolitical.

Many people admired LeBron for his increased involvement in issues that affect them not just the black community, but the nation in general.

He had found his voice in 2012 and it only grew louder and more forceful as he matured both on-court and off-court.

It appeared that the more he succeeded in his basketball career, the more he became vocal about his stand on different issues. When he refused to take a position on the Darfur issue, he had no championship ring under his name. He had a few individual awards, but he was not yet at the pinnacle of his career. Perhaps LeBron felt that he didn't have enough weapons in his arsenal to influence people and change their view on certain matters. He might even be fearful of the backlash he would receive if, God forbid, he makes an unpopular stand.

When he started winning championships, he became surer of himself. He just waited to secure his status and legacy as a professional athlete before he amped up his social activism. Winning two rings for Miami and one for Cleveland sure boosted his confidence and increased his ability to influence. He felt that more people, especially younger kids, looked up to him as a role model they can emulate and aspire to be. His responsibilities have expanded to other things, beyond basketball and beyond business ventures.

When LeBron joined the Los Angeles Lakers in 2018, the tragic mass shooting in Thousand Oaks, California was still fresh from everyone's mind. Twelve people were killed in the shooting. The Lakers and the Hawks stood united as they donned black shirts that had the word "ENOUGH" on the front and the names of the victims on the back. It didn't stop there. LeBron offered his prayers to the victims and their family and he made his views known on the issue of gun violence.

LeBron didn't care if people would hate him for his opinions. He was not afraid of the backlash from his critics. He said his piece and he didn't think about what it would do to his career. He was secured enough to ignore the noise and focus on the real issue at hand.

When he left Cleveland for the first time, his enlightenment and activism accelerated. It was a transformation that extended beyond basketball. Leaving Cleveland was not only a basketball decision that forced the NBA's power dynamics to shift from league to players, but it was also a punch in the face of team owners and general managers.

It sent shockwaves not just to the NBA but to American professional sports system. There was this young black man deciding for himself what he thought was good for him. Instead of letting white team owners decide his fortune and his future, LeBron took it upon himself to design his own destiny.

Many Cleveland fans were angered by his decision to join Miami because they only chose to see what was on the surface. They failed to understand what it truly represents, especially when it is viewed through the prism of being a black person in a league decidedly controlled by white men.

The only thing they saw was LeBron chasing rings and lining up his pockets by getting a bigger paycheck and more endorsement deals. What they failed to see was that LeBron was changing a system that was run by owners and general managers who wielded total control and power over the players.

In fact, LeBron challenged the flawed system by rebuffing the traditional representation structure in the NBA. He pulled away from the usual agent-player dynamics and instead opted to build his own agency with three friends he trusted with his life.

LeBron learned to become more assertive when it came to decisions concerning his life, business, and family. Not everyone agreed with his new style because it was viewed as greedy and being self-absorbed. The more he asserted himself, the more hate he got. This was amplified when he moved to Miami and left Cleveland without giving the city the championship ring that it sought.☐

LeBron's activism was criticized, largely because the race card is always brought up in every action he takes even when many viewed it as business and self-promotion. The system and the structure that he challenged in the NBA were within the realm of business, but the race issue was like a dark cloud hovering in a perfect sky.

No one was more displeased by the sudden shift in power other than those who wielded the power for so long—the white men and women who owned the teams and called the shots as they pertain to the careers of the professional athletes in the NBA, which are predominantly black. So, of course, everyone would see LeBron's move as racially motivated.

When the structure and the hierarchy are blatantly controlled by white men in a league where there are more black players than white, it is impossible to ignore the racial component that comes with it.

LeBron has never denied that he was advocating

for black rights and racial justice every time he spoke on social media or show up with in statement shirts during warmups. He intentionally used his celebrity status and his popularity to make a change, or at least move people to do something to change the circumstances of their lives. □

He drowned out the negative criticisms and focused on his advocacies. He focused more on the black kids and how to give them the opportunities to become the next great athlete, scientist, educator, or innovator. He knew what it was like to be on the other side of the fence and he was one of the lucky few who triumphed over the adversities in life. Not everyone could say the same thing. That's why he wanted the black kids to have the same opportunities he was given as a child. All he asked was to give the black kids a fighting chance to succeed in life and not be swallowed by the flawed system.

LeBron's social activism found a powerful platform in social media. He had not always been very active in social media. In fact, for seven years, he had this tradition on going dark and silent on social media to drown out the noise and eliminate distractions so he could focus on his game and other things that mattered to him. But that has changed when he saw the impact of social media, especially when it is used to achieve a goal.

Although LeBron's advocacies were largely focused on black communities, he wanted to create a universal impact. It's not just about empowering blacks but also people of other color and those that are struggling in life. His Foundation and other advocacy groups that he is affiliated with can only reach and serve so many people. But with social media, his reach would be exponential. He felt that it is his duty to use his platform to create awareness of social and political issues and help others as a result of that action.

He turned to Twitter to voice out his opinions on different issues, especially on gun violence, racial discrimination, and social injustice. He didn't hold back in his tweets. Unlike some celebrities who allow other people to manage their social media accounts, LeBron was hands-on. Twitter became an extension of himself. He spoke from the heart and his followers saw the raw emotions and the genuine empathy that he had for the families and victims of the racially-motivated hate crimes.

In 2015, he expressed his anger and frustration when an infant was killed from gunfire in Cleveland. But his tweets were more than just venting and reacting; they were also a call to action to do something. He would challenge those who are in the position to create change to take action.

It was hard to ignore a call to action from someone as big as LeBron James. With over 41 million followers on Twitter, he was a force to be reckoned with. Those who are at the receiving end of his ire would feel the deep impact and may succumb to the enormous pressure to make sweeping changes in whatever issue is being talked about at a particular point in time.

With Twitter's ability to amplify each tweet through sharing, messages can go viral in seconds. With such power to spread information, LeBron found the perfect platform to spread his own brand of advocacy. It was no longer just about LeBron the basketball superstar, but it was LeBron the social activist who wants to make an impact and create change, big or small.

LeBron continued his Twitter activism and called for greater regulation of guns and firearms. But he wasn't idealistic. He knew the impossibility of taking all the guns out, so he called for stricter laws and penalties for carrying firearms because he believed that people would think twice if there are grave consequences if they disobey the law.

Lebron was also one of the many professional athletes who was enraged by the killing of Alton Sterling by two Baton Rogue cops. He hashtagged #BlackLivesMatter in support of the movement.

Whether his Twitter activism was directly helping the cause is something that cannot be measured or quantified, but he certainly made a difference by creating awareness. With a huge following, he made an impact because his messages were amplified by those who supported him.

Conversely, those who didn't agree with him criticized him and tried to make him look incompetent. One of his biggest critics was none other than President Donald J. Trump himself. Trump had always admired LeBron and had nothing but good things to say about him as evidenced by his tweets about the superstar in 2013.

But Trump changed his stance drastically by calling LeBron the "dumbest man on television". This was in reference to LeBron's CNN interview hosted by Don Lemon. In the interview, LeBron said that Trump was using sports to divide the nation.

Even before the interview, LeBron had been

critical of the president, but surprisingly, Trump never hit back. It turned out, he was waiting for the right moment to stage his attack on LeBron and it was during an interview where much of the discussion was focused on the opening of LeBron's school for the underprivileged children.

NBA players Karl-Anthony Towns, Donovan Mitchell, and Anthony Tolliver leaped to the defense of their NBA brother. Even the great Michael Jordan was vocal of his support to LeBron and for what he does for the black and underprivileged community. Overnight, LeBron became Trump's most influential adversary who stood up to him without fear of backlash or reprisal. □

LeBron is not the type of person who would be pressured into taking a stand just because it was a popular one. He made this clear when he showed his support for the defiant San Francisco 49ers quarterback Colin Kaepernick by defending his right for a peaceful protest. Kaepernick is infamous for taking the knee during the singing of the national anthem. It was his way to protest racial inequality and police brutality.

LeBron continued his support for Kaepernick despite the backlash. In fact, he and Kevin Durant showed up to their respective games wearing #ImWithKap jerseys ahead of the Superbowl LIII weekend.

Twitter was not the only platform that LeBron used for his social activism. He turned his Instagram feed into a platform where the young generation of activists can have their voice amplified and reach millions of young followers.

LeBron is usually silent during the postseason. It has always been an annual tradition of some sort to eliminate negative distractions. He calls that tradition the "Zero Dark Thirty-23 Mode". He had done so for the past seven years until he decided that his tradition needed a little bit of tweaking.

Although LeBron remained silent in social media, his Instagram account did not. He handed his

Instagram to the next generation of social influencers who are doing amazing things in their communities to spark change and be better citizens of the country.

It may sound like a haphazard marketing strategy that just attached LeBron's name to it to gain tremendous traction and it was—and there's nothing wrong with that. The thing is that it must be put in perspective to understand the sheer genius of the strategy cooked up by LeBron.

LeBron has over 46 million followers on Instagram. That puts him the fifth most followed professional athlete on Instagram, just trailing football superstars Ronaldo, Messi, Neymar, and David Beckham. To put that in perspective, his following is double the population of every NBA playoff team's home city combined. Furthermore, Game 1 of the Eastern Conference finals between the Cleveland Cavaliers and the Boston Celtics drew over 7.2 million viewers on ABC. That's a lot of ready audience that LeBron can tap into. Simply put, it's huge!

The opportunity to make a difference was already there, all it needed was a strong platform where young people could show what they were doing that could inspire and spark change even in small ways.

The result was an amazing showcase of stories from teenagers and young adults that highlighted their experiences with business success, social justice, or philanthropy.

Instagram Story was the perfect platform to do this. Every 24 hours, a new story is posted. Even if only a fraction of LeBron's followers watched it, it would make a difference in somebody's life. That's how powerful social media is in the hands of a popular superstar like LeBron.

LeBron's activism was not limited to social and political issues. His influence and impact reverberated in the NBA. In 2013, he ruffled the owners and managers' feathers when he spoke out against the lack of revenue sharing in the league. This was triggered when it was reported that the Sacramento Kings was getting sold for $525 million.

The NBA has a form of revenue sharing, but it is not included in Basketball Related Income (BRI). The exclusion has to do with the calculation of the salary cap. It poses an economic advantage to big market teams and drive the salary cap up which would force teams in small markets to spend more money just to retain their players, especially their All-Stars and superstars. It is not sustainable for the small markets and it creates economic disparity among franchises. It impacts the league negatively.

Although it is clear that revenue sharing is a complex problem that cannot be resolved in the immediate future, what LeBron was pointing out was that there is money to be shared even if the owners are saying otherwise.

LeBron even considered running for president of the NBA Players Association (NBPA) in the same year just to give players a strong and powerful leader in helping voice their grievances. Although it didn't come into fruition on that year, he was elected as vice president in 2015, two years after his initial interest in getting involved in the player union. He was the first vice president of that association and was elected unanimously by the players, which showed how much the players believed in his ability to negotiate.

LeBron became interested in the position because he wanted to influence negotiations over television deals and other issues relating to player contracts. Plus, with the way the league was being run, LeBron sensed that there could be another potential labor struggle in 2017 akin to the 2011 NBA lockout that led to the 161-day work stoppage. This was due to the players union opting out for the collective bargaining agreement.

The union was fighting for a larger portion of the potential multi-billion revenue that the NBA was expected to earn in light of the massive $24 billion television deal it secured. LeBron's presence in the NBPA gave the players' union extra leverage to get the increased salary cap and the best deals.

LeBron comfortably transitioned into his role and the players supported him 100 percent. The players knew that his involvement in negotiations would help them get the kind of deals that they truly deserved and not to be dictated by the league and the team owners.

Many of his critics came to view LeBron's involvement as a way to get more money for the players whose salaries had been consistently on the rise. They said that his motivations were purely for financial advantage—short of saying that LeBron was a megalomaniac who wanted more. What they failed to see was that LeBron was looking after the welfare of the players. He got involved because he wanted to change the system.

The NBA's balance of power skewed in favor of owners and general managers. A player's fate had always been decided by team executives who were in collusion with the league leadership. The players were always at the mercy of the owners. This was the flawed system that LeBron wanted to change. He wanted players to hold the key to their own future. His own free agency was the model to which NBA players are utilizing to plan their careers. It's a long way to go before the league relinquishes some of its power to tilt the balance to the players' favor, but LeBron showed the league that the players hold the power to make or break the league.

Chapter 4
- The Mogul -

After the embarrassing sweep of the Cleveland Cavaliers in the hands of the defending champions Golden State Warriors, LeBron's future in Cleveland became uncertain. Many were convinced that the devastating loss was the last straw and LeBron was ready to move on from Cleveland. After all, he already delivered his promise to give Cleveland a championship ring. What more could the city ask for?

LeBron's free agency kicked off on July 1, 2018. The NBA offseason became a big reality show filled with speculations, maneuverings, and drama. Teams that had enough salary cap space were in contention to land the greatest NBA player of this generation.

The Los Angeles Lakers had the most salary cap space at $62 million—enough to sign LeBron and one more All-Star free agent like Paul George, Chris Paul, Kevin Durant, or Demarcus Cousins.

Philadelphia was an option but the odds were not in their favor because other than rising stars Joel Embid and Ben Simmons, the 76ers didn't have much to offer. The "Process" lost steam in the 2018 Eastern Conference semifinals and bowed to the Boston Celtics in five games.

The Houston Rockets, the Boston Celtics, and the San Antonio Spurs were also potential landing spots.

Cleveland could match any offer other teams made and could make LeBron $205 million richer if he re-signed. His legacy was already secured in Cleveland so he didn't need to prove himself to the city. With the locker room and management relationship becoming more strained each day, staying for another two years could only create a more toxic environment.

Unlike his 2010 free agency, LeBron did not have the need for elaborate pitch meetings. Fifteen years in the league was more than enough to know what each team could offer him. As the deadline drew close, it became apparent that his eyes were set on Los Angeles. But despite this, the announcement still sent shockwaves through the NBA and the world. Cleveland had lost its son for the second time.

Those who had closely followed LeBron's career progression already knew that the move to Los Angeles was inevitable. It was the logical decision considering how LeBron was preparing himself after he retires. Many people think that his decisions to move from one team to the next was to chase championship rings and catchup with Michael Jordan and Kobe Bryant.

What was not obvious to a lot of people was that LeBron had already started using his global popularity to create an entertainment empire. He was not quite there yet like Magic Johnson or Michael Jordan, but he had the right resources and people that could get him there. The move to the Los Angeles Lakers was not just about basketball and championships. In to his mid-30s, LeBron is still in peak game shape. He is still hungry for more championship rings and individual accolades. But he is always hungry for more and his ambition diversified into other things. He wanted to conquer the entertainment world as well. And there's no better city to build an entertainment empire in other than Los Angeles.

People should have seen this coming, but they were too stuck in basketball to notice LeBron's burgeoning entertainment career. In 2008, LeBron co-founded a production company called SpringHill Entertainment, named after the housing complex that LeBron and his mother moved into when he was in sixth grade.

Together with his childhood friend, Maverick Carter, LeBron developed a number of TV shows and documentaries under the fledgling production company. The company is slated to do a remake of House Party, a remake of the 1990 hip hop comedy show. Rumor swirled around for years about a possible remake of the cult classic *Space Jam*, but it never happened—at least not yet in the early years of the production company.

In 2015, SpringHill launched the sports-themed *Uninterrupted,* a digital video platform that features shows, documentaries, and content created by professional athletes. It paved the way for bigger projects when Warner Brothers partnered with SpringHill and invested $16 million in the platform to develop TV, film, and digital products.

To date, the production company's portfolio includes the Disney series *Becoming,* Starz's dramedy *Survivor's Remorse*, an NBC trivia game show pilot, and *Uninterrupted* for Turner's Bleacher Report. In the pipeline is a CNBC show about transforming businesses on the brink of collapse. It will have LeBron and Carter in the show. They are also in talks with NBCUniversal about potential shows that will feature LeBron.

In September 2018, the production company announced that LeBron would be suiting up for the Tune Squad for the sequel of Space Jam, to be directed by Black Panther director Ryan Coogler. *Space Jam* was the 1996 hit film that starred Michael Jordan. The live-action movie became a cult classic mainly due to Jordan's team up with Bugs Bunny and the Looney Tunes squad. It was Jordan's first foray into acting—something extra to put in his impressive list of accomplishments and the one thing that LeBron didn't have until he appeared in the movie *Trainwreck* with Amy Schumer.

LeBron made a splash in his first acting gig and earned rave reviews for his impressive comedic timing. Everyone harped on how natural he was in acting and wondered if he would consider it a post-basketball career. He signed with William Morris Endeavor Agency (WME) and is represented by Ari Manuel to handle his career in the entertainment space. Manuel is the agent that handles Mark Wahlberg, which says so much about his caliber when it comes to project and salary negotiations.

Manuel had already worked with LeBron and Carter in 2010 with the ESPN special *The Decision*, the television special which announced LeBron's decision to sign with the Miami Heat instead of taking Cleveland's offer and staying in his hometown when he became a free agent.

Director Judd Apatow had nothing but nice things to say about LeBron. Apatow had apprehensions on how someone of LeBron's stature would feel about certain scenes. He feared that LeBron would not be game to have fun and try new things. He's known for doing a lot of improvisations in his movies, so it was a baptism of fire of some sort for Lebron. As it turned out, he was really good at improvisation and the result was a fun and hilarious romp.

LeBron has always been honest about his plans. He made it very clear that he wants his post-basketball career to be in Hollywood. He has a rare combination of talent, business savvy, appeal, and popularity to make it big in the entertainment business. He looked to the successful career of Magic Johnson after retiring from professional basketball as the business blueprint he wanted to follow. If his acting career thrives, he can be likened to Dwayne "The Rock" Johnson, who leveraged his wrestling career to land plum roles in big-budgeted Hollywood films.

At 34, the choice to move to Los Angeles and don the purple and gold uniform were in line with his vision to build an entertainment empire befitting his stature, persona, and values. While his basketball career is still at peak level, LeBron is already exploring new entertainment opportunities that Hollywood has to offer.

What not many people know is that LeBron had already dipped his hand in the Hollywood cookie jar back in 2008. He is close friends with Jimmy Iovine, who is the co-founder of Beats Electronic and Interscope Records. The friendship stemmed from a business partnership when LeBron became an investor in Beats and Iovine produced *More Than a Game*, a documentary about LeBron's high school basketball career.

LeBron knew a thing or two about the business even before he decided to be more involved in the negotiations and production. He was taking things slowly and gradually learning the tricks of the trade by how he interacted with established names and companies in the business. He is smart about his money and even smarter with the people he does business with. He knew right from the start that not anyone can be trusted when it comes to money and career. So, he surrounded himself with people he can trust—Maverick Carter, Rich Paul, and Randy Mims.

When LeBron announced his decision to leave Cleveland for Miami in 2010, Carter, Paul, and Mims were heavily criticized and ridiculed for the TV special "The Decision." Everyone thought it was a stupid way to announce it and utterly disrespectful to Cleveland Cavaliers' owner Dan Gilbert, management, coaches and players. But more than that, it was a betrayal of the highest degree to the millions of Cavaliers fans who supported him and treated him like a son.

The traditional route would have been to inform the Cleveland Cavaliers management about his decision to leave and then issue a press release. LeBron did not do both. Instead, he and three of his best friends turned it into a media circus—at least that was how many people perceived it. Just by taking it at face value, one would think that it was LeBron's idea. It would appear egotistical and self-serving. However, the idea came from American journalist and sportscaster Jim Gray, who pitched the idea to Carter, LeBron's agent and childhood friend. To refresh one's memory, Gray was the reporter who made an ambush interview with Pete Rose and grilled him about gambling allegations. This was right after the Cincinnati Reds slugger was selected by fans to the All-Century Team. Suffice to say, Gray has a penchant for controversy and scandal. He's the type to disturb a beehive just to get the ultimate scoop.□

If people knew the real story, they wouldn't be so quick with the criticisms and judgment. But no one knew until the decision was scrutinized and criticized in every aspect. There was no way to look at it but a publicity disaster that hurt LeBron's legacy more than anything else. But he didn't get the brunt of the backlash. Carter, Paul, and Mims were crucified for even considering Gray's idea. Many said that if somebody more experienced and more PR savvy were handling LeBron's affairs, it would have taken a different turn.

Carter went on record to say that he got onboard with the idea because of the fundraising component of it—ESPN actually agreed to donate the time while the sponsors pledged $3 million, which Nike matched dollar for dollar. Proceeds of the fundraising would benefit the Boys and Girls Clubs of America.

In hindsight, the opportunity to raise funds for charity is always a good thing, but it only played a minor role and was never the main event. In that aspect, Carter became a victim of the very same people that he should be protecting LeBron against.

The lack of experience in dealing with these kinds of negotiations was what many of LeBron's critics warned about when he fired his agent and replaced him with Carter. The critics were right in questioning Carter's qualifications and they felt that they proved their point when the publicity stunt backfired. As a result, LeBron was the most hated man in Cleveland at that particular point in time.

Observers pointed out that during the airing of *The Decision,* LeBron was uncharacteristically nervous and uncomfortable. Many said that he must have realized how bad the idea was and couldn't hide it.

If it were any other agent or manager, he or she would have been fired right there and then, but it was not the case with Carter and friends. LeBron's loyalty is to his friends. He knew it was a mistake and while it cannot be rectified, the next decisions should be better.

As for Carter, he got caught in the middle of a media maelstrom, all because he was sold on the idea of helping raise funds for charity. He paid for it by getting the flak and LeBron paid for it for not thinking things through. The press and the media got the scandal and controversy that they wanted and the issue was media fodder for days.

It was unequivocally a terrible start to build a Hollywood empire. Clearly, LeBron and Carter had a lot to learn in terms of business maneuverings. This is all the more reason that LeBron needed Carter, Paul, and Mims on his side because people in the business can be manipulative but they hide their real intentions under the guise of fundraising for charity.

The LeBron James' brand and image were hurt in the process, but LeBron did not take it sitting down. He knew that they had to put the mistake behind them and move on. There was no point in damage control; they needed to be smarter and be better.

By now, the drama of The Decision had long been forgotten after LeBron returned to Cleveland after two years of absence and delivered the championship ring to his beloved hometown. Time and the championship ring had erased the bad memories. LeBron had settled the score and made amends with his Cleveland fans. So, when he left Cleveland for the second time for a greener pasture in Los Angeles, Cleveland understood. There were no hard feelings—not when the King gave his subjects the one thing that it wanted more than anything in the world.

After the circus that was *The Decision,* LeBron moved on and focused on playing basketball and he led the Cavaliers back to its back-to-back NBA finals appearance in 2018. Everywhere LeBron went, controversy hounded him, but he always found a way to drown out the noise. Locker room upheaval and a massive multiplayer trade have affected the team dynamics and contributed to their fall—yet again—to the mighty and solid Golden State Warriors squad.

Eight years after the much-derided TV special, LeBron and his three friends are still together. While other friendships would break from the pressure, Lebron's friendship with Carter, Paul, and Mims grew even stronger. LeBron chose his friends over established talent agencies because he knew he was in good and capable hands. He didn't succumb to the pressure from the media and critics who advised him that he should surround himself with more experienced people to help him transition to the businessman lifestyle.

The "Four Horsemen," as they had been called, stuck to their guns and kept their heads held high. They continue to help LeBron realize his dreams and prove their detractors wrong. With the way things are working out, they are starting to get the respect.

LeBron's ambition to build a Hollywood empire included his friends. His dreams were also their dreams. Despite the difficulties and adversities in navigating the entertainment industry, they kept going, making mistakes along the way but learning from them.

In the eight years that they've been together as business partners, they had established an impressive portfolio. Apart from the mainstream projects that had them working with big studios, they have created quality documentaries that were considered raw, honest, and real.

One docuseries that SpringHill produced was *More Than an Athlete.* It chronicled the four men's journey from the streets of Akron to the global stage. It was the first time Carter, Paul, and Mims had equal billing with LeBron. They were allowed to show the success they achieved and the heights they have reached. Each of them was given the chance to shine with LeBron as the human platform to reach the goals they have set out for themselves.

Each has a role to play in building the Hollywood Empire that LeBron envisioned. LeBron knew he could not do it alone but he made sure that he was around positive individuals who are motivated and driven to succeed. LeBron knew that Carter, Paul, and Mims were the right guys before they realized they were the right guys. They were the backcourt generals who made sure things are working like clockwork while LeBron does his LeBron things on the court and off the court.

As the CEO of SpringHill Entertainment, Carter manages LeBron's business interests. He is the leader on the business side of things. Mims is LeBron's Chief of Staff and travels with him to take care of other business ventures. Paul is LeBron's agent who has made a name for himself in the realm of sports agency. He also represents superstars and risings stars under the Klutch Sports—Anthony Davis, Ben Simmons, John Wall, Tristan Thompson, J.R. Smith, and Eric Bledsoe, among others.

The four of them felt that it was important to tell their story, not to redeem themselves from the mistakes of the past, but to inspire people to keep reaching for the stars because dreams are attainable with hard work, determination, and the right mindset. They wanted to show that the road to success is not linear. It leads to different paths and has stops and starts at any point of the journey. There are sacrifices that come along and there are risks to take.

When they created the docuseries, they were hoping that people would be inspired and empowered. With LeBron as the brand and the platform, it was not difficult to send the uplifting message that anything is possible if every person is given the fighting chance to succeed in life. They are living proof that even four guys from Akron can make it big. Sometimes it just takes a little push, a little motivation to start something special.

What is clear from the get-go is that they are capitalizing on LeBron's popularity, appeal, and influence to establish a unique entertainment empire that can help solidify LeBron's footprint as a legitimate influential business mogul in Hollywood.

Many of SpringHill's projects are more in line with LeBron evolving as a person—to show the world that he is more than a basketball superstar. Something has awakened inside of him that made him more socially-conscious and politically astute.

In HBO's *The Shop,* LeBron goes candid and unscripted together with his famous friends including Odell Beckham, Jr., Drake, Snoop Dog, and Candace Parker, to name a few. They talk about adulthood, racial expectations, and other important issues that affect them in a barbershop where they can share their points of view freely and uninterrupted. They are showing the human side of celebrities that people can relate to. It makes viewers realize that their popularity and stature do not exempt them from hardships in life. It's a great insight into the minds of people who were given the opportunity to change their lives because someone believed in them.

This is the kind of content LeBron wants to bring to mainstream consciousness. Many topics are usually off-limits on television and LeBron wants to change that and have an open discussion and a healthy exchange of opinions and insights. ☐

LeBron is not only using social media to promote his brand and image, but he is also using traditional media to create social awareness. He is linking his brand to important issues so that they can enter people's consciousness and form their own opinions about them.

Although it's hardly groundbreaking, LeBron's approach is unique and very much in sync with the social climate. It not only creates content that is relatable, but it also creates an opportunity to empower viewers and inspire them to take action.

LeBron's road to "mogulhood" is paved with good intention. He is combining different aspects of his life to build something that can potentially improve the lives of other people. His basketball career is closely linked to his philanthropic efforts and his business ventures. The man, the brand, and the advocacy are interspersed and impossible to separate. So, with every endeavor, whether it's business-driven, marketing-driven, or advocacy-driven, it always leads to the achievement of a goal that leads to a profound and meaningful change to an individual, a community, or a population.

Chapter 5
- The Philanthropist -

Lebron's social and political awakening came a little late and it was triggered by a tragic event, but he was no stranger to the hardships and turmoil in life. He experienced first-hand how it is to live with a single parent who lives on paycheck to paycheck. He had lost count of how many times they had to move from one housing complex to the next. He had to live with a family just so he could have a permanent address and have the opportunity to play basketball. He understood poverty and scarcity. He lived it most of his young life. The least he could do was to give back to the community that believed in him and made him who he is.

It's no secret that LeBron's impoverished upbringing is the motivation for his philanthropic efforts. Most professional athletes who are given multimillion-dollar contracts donate to their charities of choice and move on. It's something they are expected to do and they do rise to the occasion. For LeBron, he wanted to give back in a big way. He wants something concrete, sustainable, and long-lasting.

LeBron values education and he believes that it can positively impact the lives of underprivileged children and young adults. With a clear mission in mind, LeBron established The LeBron James Family Foundation.

The Foundation is more than just a platform to raise and donate money to charitable organizations. It's the perfect conduit to which his ultimate philanthropic goal can materialize. It's where he can build and secure his off-court legacy.

The philanthropic work that LeBron does through his foundation is not just simply supporting charities financially, it is changing the lives of young children who are given the opportunity to get an education. Although LeBron's philanthropic work is far-reaching, Akron holds a special place in his heart. Much of the efforts are put towards helping the communities in Akron and other inner cities that needed help.

Even before LeBron made it big in the NBA, he was already helping in any way he could with the resources he had. The loftier goals of the Foundation came much later when he reached superstar status and he had the means to support charitable groups from his own pocket.

The Foundation started the After-School All-Stars in his hometown in Akron, Ohio. It raised and donated money to benefit the children in Akron. One of the most important projects that LeBron spearheaded was the Wheels for Education. The project raised money to ensure that the children of Akron can have an education and a place to go to after school. The aim is to keep them off the streets and away from the lure of bad elements like drugs, gangs, and crime.

At-risk children in Akron are being mentored so that they get the extra help that they need to succeed in school. They are also given opportunities to excel in extracurricular activities by letting them get involved and have the necessary interaction that can lead to an healthy social development. Keeping the kids at school encourages them to graduate. They are given incentives to stay and learn. LeBron believes that if the kids are given a sense of purpose, they will develop a deep commitment to finish their education. When they are educated, they can go on and do the things they want to do and achieve their dreams.

The project begins in the third grade when children are required to reach the state standards so they could move on to the fourth grade. Specifically, the program provides tutoring and mentoring in math and reading. Those who are having difficulties at school are provided with help so that they don't get discouraged and drop out. In the long run, it gives the kids the tools they need to succeed not just in school but in life.

The Foundation has raised more than $40 million for the program. The program was a massive success that it got the University of Akron involved and offered scholarships to deserving students. Parents were encouraged to participate so that they can see how their children are progressing in school and in their extracurricular activities. □

The success of the program is mainly due to LeBron's involvement and hands-on approach. He was always interacting with the kids in the program and providing them with support and inspiration. His constant presence shows the children that he is serious and committed to the cause. The kids see LeBron's genuine involvement in the program. When he cannot be around the kids, he connects with them in social media.

With the partnership with the University of Akron, the scholarship covers about $9500 in college tuition for every student in the program, which has over 800 children. The first graduating class under the scholarship program will graduate in 2021. With the tremendous success of the program, LeBron hopes to widen its reach throughout the state of Ohio and even extend it to other states.

Aside from outreach programs and charity projects, LeBron also donates money to institutions and charitable organizations whose goals are in line with his own philanthropic goals. He had donated $2.5 million for the exhibit at the Smithsonian National Museum of African and American History and Culture honoring the boxing great Muhammad Ali.

LeBron has said that Muhammad Ali was a big inspiration for him as an athlete. Ali's philosophies about sports and discipline became guiding principles to LeBron which influenced how he approached sports and competition. But more than that, LeBron credits Ali for being a champion of justice who helped influence the Civil Rights Movement.

The Boys and Girls Club of America always has a special place in LeBron's heart. Growing up, LeBron considered it a safe haven. It was a home away from home and helped him stay out of trouble. He said that it is places like Boys and Girls Club that help kids learn and grow during their formative years. He donated the proceeds of ESPN's *The Decision* to the Club.

LeBron really empathizes with at-risk children and he wanted to help alleviate the problems that these children face on a daily basis. This is why LeBron supports non-profit organizations like the Children's Defense Fund which have programs that focus on child advocacy so that children can thrive and reach their full potential even in the face of adversities.

Because the After-School All-Stars largely operates in Akron, its reach is very limited. By donating to the Children's Defense Fund, LeBron's help can extend to other places that his own Foundation cannot reach. The Fund's goals align with LeBron's own goals because they focus on helping children from poor backgrounds complete their education and finish college.

ONEXONE is another organization that focuses on helping and taking care of children. LeBron's Foundation is a major contributor to the organization because the program gives back to the children in immeasurable ways. It ensures that children are provided with basic necessities like food, water, and shelter. Aside from educational help and after school activities, the organization also provides medical help to those who need it.

Lebron's ultimate philanthropic dream came true when he opened the I Promise School. It is the culmination of years of hard work and research. It had humble beginnings through the Foundation's I Promise Program but it can potentially change the way how public school is being run and delivered not just in Akron, but also across the country.

Many were quick to dismiss I Promise School as

just a marketing vehicle to promote the LeBron James brand. Some say that it's one of those "Next Big Idea" in education that is all hyped up but loses its steam and flatlines as soon as the publicity stops. LeBron addressed the issue and assured everyone that the I Promise School is not some fad that's doomed to fail. The idea is not new or revolutionary, but it will change lives for the better.

The I Promise School's blueprint reveals an unorthodox approach to public school teaching. It is first and foremost designed as a public school. It specifically targets students from Akron Public School who still struggle despite the existing support extended to them. Majority of the kids from Akron go to public schools because of poverty so it just makes complete sense to make I Promise a part of the Akron public school system.

When it opened on July 30, 2018, it welcomed 240 students in the third and fourth grades. It is committed to educating the children and encouraging them to finish education. It's projected to grow and serve children from grades one through eight by the year 2022.

The five-year plan of the I Promise School can be considered ambitious because it wants to be the top urban school system in America. What's unique about this is that it has explicit goals of improving everyone in the community. All the residents of Akron stand to benefit, not just the students.

The curriculum, assignments and classroom instructions are grounded in the development of Akron. LeBron believes that if children are taught to value the community they are in, they will be encouraged to commit to local efforts to build inclusive and socially just neighborhoods.

The master plan for the I Promise School is that education is not limited to academics. Teaching should touch on every aspect of a student's life. Often times, students are equipped to deal with school work and academic load, but they lack the emotional, mental, and psychological maturity to deal with real-world issues. As such, programs that help children regulate their emotions, interact with others, and develop self-awareness are incorporated in the curriculum. LeBron believes that if a public school can educate the whole child, he or she will be ready to face life's challenges that come with being black or underserved or underprivileged.

The I Promise School is bigger than anything that LeBron has achieved on-court. By giving back to the people of Akron and taking care of the underprivileged children of his hometown, his life has come full circle. He has made a mark in Akron and in the world with his basketball, but his greatness is not measured in championship rings, but in what he has given back to his community.

Chapter 6
- The Future -

The future is bright for LeBron when he signed a four-year $154 million contract with the Los Angeles Lakers in 2018. This is particularly special for him because the decision is not solely about basketball. The lure of the purple and gold was strong because of the impressive history of winning. Many of the basketball greats like Kareem Abdul-Jabbar, Magic Johnson, and Kobe Bryant have brought championship rings to the city and there is a big pressure for LeBron to deliver one. He has plenty of time to do it, but knowing LeBron's winning ways, everything can be expedited—one title goal can easily swing to multiple titles in four years.

By switching to a new team, LeBron is building a case for being the best in the current league or perhaps of all time. All he needed are the right pieces to make the Lakers true title contenders. The team just needs to reach the playoffs. The last time the Lakers were in the playoffs was in 2013. The pressure is on but LeBron is prepared to rise to the challenge.

LeBron's move to Los Angeles is, first and foremost, a business decision. His ambition to build an entertainment empire has the best chance of coming to fruition in Hollywood. He's still good for four years of professional basketball, but he is already securing his position as an entertainment mogul.

LeBron's decision also impacts his family. His wife Savannah James has always been LeBron's support system throughout his career. He needs her now more than ever at this point in his career. Their kids LeBron, Jr., Maximus, and Zhuri are growing up and the family dynamics are bound to change. LeBron, Jr. is following in his father's footsteps and has the makings of a basketball superstar.

LeBron has to balance career, business, and family life while he and his family adjust to a new city and a new set of challenges. It's no secret that LeBron is nearing the final era of his playing career and he is slowly transitioning to other lofty endeavors. No one knows what the future would bring, but LeBron's legacy is already set and it's a legacy that's hard to match.

Chapter 7
- Life Lessons and Blueprint
to Success -

Everything that LeBron James touches turns to gold. He can very well be the modern-day Midas. With his enormous paycheck and multimillion-dollar endorsement deals, it's hard to imagine that LeBron once lived in poverty. It's almost unthinkable that his entire childhood is filled with struggles and hardships. But that is all behind him now.

With his God-given talent, he was given the opportunity of a lifetime. What he did with that opportunity was so remarkable that he catapulted himself to greater heights and gave back to the community that nurtured him and made him who he is today.

LeBron's remarkable athletic ability and on-court vision made him one of the greatest basketball players to ever grace the NBA. He achieved greatness because he is always challenging himself to do better. Every time he achieves a milestone in life, he finds ways to be better. It's a never-ending quest for perfection and excellence in everything he does whether it be in basketball or other things.

LeBron succeeded in every endeavor he set his eyes on because he always has a game plan. He accomplished things that only a few people can do because he always seems to find solutions to problems or always one step ahead when it comes to decision-making. All these contributed to his success.

By understanding and knowing LeBron beyond the realm of basketball, one can find a wealth of life lessons and a blueprint for success.

1. Find something you love to do and put your heart and soul into it.

LeBron is passionate about basketball. He had a talent for it in the beginning, but he didn't become great overnight. He worked hard and put his heart and soul into improving his craft. Even after 16 years of playing in the NBA, he is still as passionate about the game as he was the first time he set foot on the court.

2. Surround yourself with people you trust and make you better.

When LeBron decided that he wanted to build a business empire in Los Angeles, he surrounded himself with childhood friends and people who were with him when he was still dirt poor. He hired friends to be his agent, chief of staff, and business manager because he knew that they would look after his interests. The result is a burgeoning entertainment media company that is making a splash in the digital media realm.

3. Keep Improving

LeBron has evolved as a player throughout the years. When he was drafted in 2003, he was all that the press said he would be in the NBA. He had powerful dunks, remarkable ball-handling skills, and great athleticism, but his jump shot was lacking. He worked on his jump shot and became a clutch shooter. When his post-up game was criticized, he worked on it as well and became a solid threat in post-up plays.

4. Adapt to the Changes

Gameplay and play style in the NBA changed drastically over the years that's why some players cannot cope and leave the league prematurely. LeBron knew that to have a long and successful career in the NBA, he had to adapt to the changes. He developed new skills and new shoots, and constantly moved with the times. He kept himself in game shape so he could compete with new player fresh legs and mean streaks.

Even in business and other undertakings, LeBron embraced change. He was quick to use social media as a platform to promote not just his brand but also his advocacies. His online presence in social media made his brand more popular and accessible.□

5. Never Forget Where You Came From

No matter how hard life was growing up in Akron, LeBron never forgets the place. It has a special place in his heart because it was the place that shaped his morals, ideals, and values. Akron has been very good to him when he succeeded and he was returning the favor by improving the community and empowering the residents.

6. Make the People Around You Better

LeBron's teammates perform better when he is around. This is a fact and statistics would prove it. Many of them played their best in seasons when LeBron was making the plays. It's no secret that LeBron creates plays that put his teammates in the best position to shoot the ball. He also does this in business. He put his three childhood friends in roles based on their strengths. They capitalized on those strengths and became the best business partners that LeBron could ever ask for.

7. Create Opportunities

LeBron credited the people who gave him the opportunity to succeed in life. All he needed was that one chance to prove that he could make his life better and he could become what he wanted to be. This is the very same thing that he is doing for other people in Akron. With the I Promise School, he is creating opportunities for kids who would usually be dismissed and ignored. LeBron believes that creating opportunities is a big step to changing unfavorable circumstances into positive ones.□

8. Don't Hold Grudges

When LeBron left Cleveland for Miami, fans felt betrayed. Some of them were so enraged that they burned his jersey on the streets. Cleveland Cavaliers owner Dan Gilbert penned a strongly-worded letter addressed to the fans about LeBron's betrayal. LeBron was called selfish, self-absorbed, and a traitor, among other distasteful adjectives. He had every right to bear a grudge because the negative publicity had affected his game and his mindset. But he chose not to. As time passed, when the opportunity to return to

Cleveland presented itself, he grabbed it. He and Gilbert made up and together they delivered to Cleveland their first championship in 52 years.

9. *Reframe Circumstances*

Reframing circumstances is when a person is able to transform a negative event into something positive by changing the response to the situation. LeBron's infamous decision to leave Cleveland angered the fans. Fans took it upon themselves to verbally attack or boo LeBron every time he had the ball in any game he played except in Miami.

LeBron initially engaged the fans in heated exchanges. He responded negatively to the negative situation, so it was not a surprise that it also had an adverse outcome. It affected him mentally and emotionally that his game suffered. Before he spiraled out of control, he decided to change his approach and reframe his circumstances. He turned something negative to something positive and reaped the rewards.

10. *Prepare and Research*

LeBron is not afraid of uncertainties because he trusts himself to make the right decisions even during stressful situations. He has always done his homework by researching all the possible scenarios. He knows when things might get difficult and when problems might arise. He has figured out the workarounds so that he would still succeed even when faced with seemingly insurmountable challenges.

Conclusion

I want to thank you and congratulate you for transiting my lines from start to finish.☐

I hope this book was able to help you learn from the incredible life story of LeBron James and inspire you to do better in all aspects of your life. All his achievements and successes in life are borne out of sheer determination, hard work, and a winning mindset. Luck and talent are not enough to win in life. One must be able to put the time and effort to realize dreams and achieve the same level of greatness (or even more) that LeBron has achieved.

The next step is to create opportunities out of adversities and hardships in life. Everyone is going through something, but you can turn any adverse situation into an opportunity for renewal and growth.

I wish you the best of luck!

Patrick   *Thompson*

Other Books from The Author

1) *Stephen Curry: The Inspirational Story of One of the Greatest Basketball Players of All Time!*

2) *Kobe Bryant: The Inspirational Story of One of the Greatest Basketball Players of All Time!*

Made in United States
North Haven, CT
30 October 2022

26130134R00059